DINOSAURS
DEATH AND
DISCOVERY

DOUGAL DIXON

WATTS BOOKS
London • New York • Sydney

CONTENTS

First published in the USA in 1993 by Highlights for Children, Inc.

This edition published in the UK in 1993 by Watts Books
96 Leonard Street
London EC2A 4RH

Franklin Watts Australia
14 Mars Road
Lane Cove
NSW 2066

ISBN: Hardback Edition 0 7496 1378 5
Paperback Edition 0 7496 1470 6

10 9 8 7 6 5 4 3 2 1

A CIP catalogue record for this book is available from the British Library.

The Dinosaur Series was produced for Highlights for Children, Inc. by Bender Richardson White, P.O. Box 266, Uxbridge UB9 5NX, England.

Project Editor: Lionel Bender
Art Editor: Ben White
Production: Kim Richardson
Assistant Editor: Madeleine Samuel
Typesetting and Media Conversion: Peter MacDonald & Una Macnamara

Printed in Spain

The Age of Dinosaurs

The first dinosaurs appeared about 225 million years ago (mya for short) in what scientists call the Late Triassic Period. They thrived through the following Jurassic Period and died out at the end of the Cretaceous Period 65 million years ago. During this time, geography, climate and vegetation, or plant life, were constantly changing – as shown in these dinosaur scenes.

Triassic 245–208 mya
A single giant landmass or supercontinent, mostly desert conditions, tree ferns and conifers.

Early and Middle Jurassic 208–157 mya Supercontinent, shallow seas, moist climate, tree ferns, conifers and cycads.

INTRODUCTION

When the first dinosaur bones were found, no one could explain them. They were thought to be the bones of giants, or of sinners that were killed in the great flood of the Book of Genesis in the Bible. Only in the nineteenth century did people begin to look at these fossils scientifically. They found them to be the remains of giant reptiles that walked the Earth millions of years before people existed. At first these animals were considered to be like giant lizards. As more and more remains were found, it became clearer what kinds of animals these were.

Today we have more information so that we believe we know all about these great creatures and the other living things of the past. But every year brings new discoveries. As new information is gathered, scientists come up with new theories about prehistoric life. The excitement of the study of fossil remains – a science we call palaeontology – is that our views are constantly changing and need updating. Our knowledge of the past continually develops as we move into the future. And although the dinosaurs are long dead, our picture of them is still evolving.

Late Jurassic 157–146 mya
Supercontinent beginning to break up, dry inland, moist climates by coasts.

Early Cretaceous 146–97 mya
Continents drifting into separate landmasses, plant life as in Triassic and Jurassic periods.

Late Cretaceous 97–65 mya
Separate continents, each with its own animal life, and plants like modern types.

CATASTROPHE

About 140 million years ago, a broad lake lay across much of north-west Europe. To the north of it, ridges of rock stretched from Wales to Belgium. The English Channel did not exist then. Streams cut ravines through the ridges, forming steep slopes of limestone, sandstone and coal laid down nearly 200 million years earlier. The streams flowed southward towards the lake. At the edge of the lake they spread out to form deltas – fan-shaped, muddy, swampy areas. The ravines, slopes and deltas were covered in forests of conifer trees. Ferns and cycads grew beneath the conifers, forming a thick undergrowth. Horsetails grew along the banks of the lake.

This was the landscape of the dinosaurs. Along the lake's edge and in the swamps roamed herds of the two-footed plant-eater *Iguanodon* and its small, fast-moving relative *Hypsilophodon*. Big meat-eaters such as *Baryonyx* hunted through the undergrowth. In the skies flew pterosaurs. Crocodiles and turtles wallowed in the shallow water. It was a lush landscape in which many creatures lived. Many died there as well.

Among the ravines of one of the ridges there was a depression, a giant hollow in the ground. This was frequently washed by flash floods following rainstorms. During one such flood, an *Iguanodon* was caught and drowned by the waters while crossing the river farther up, and its dead body was washed into the depression. Then another dead *Iguanodon* was washed down, and its body settled beside the first. Eventually so many dead bodies of *Iguanodon* had gathered that the hollow became a true dinosaurs' graveyard.

▷ An *Iguanodon* is carried down a gorge by a flash flood as other *Iguanodon* look on. It settles in a hollow. Minutes earlier, the *Iguanodon* was grazing on the river bank. This was the first part of the process that turned the dinosaur into remains preserved in rock – into fossils – that we can see today.

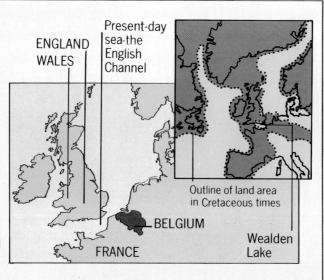

Location of the graveyard
In the Early Cretaceous Period, northern North America was joined to Europe, and a sea called the Tethys separated Europe and Africa. On the northern European continent there was a warm shallow lake called the Wealden, as on this map. Along the forested shores of this lake roamed dinosaurs like *Iguanodon*.

ENGLAND
WALES

Present-day sea-the English Channel

Outline of land area in Cretaceous times

BELGIUM

FRANCE

Wealden Lake

TIME PASSES

Within a few weeks, the soft parts of the dead bodies of the *Iguanodon* – skin, muscles, hearts, brains, stomachs, lungs and so on – rotted away. But the hard parts, the bones, did not. They stayed unchanged and still joined together as skeletons. The dead bodies of other animals lying out on open ground had been torn to bits by scavenging animals, and their bones were now broken and scattered. In the hollow, the bones of the *Iguanodon* had not been disturbed. But they had become covered by layers of mud, sand and soil laid on top of them by the river.

Over many thousands of years the landscape changed. The river wore deeper into the ridge. The ridge itself became worn down by wind, rain and ice. Sediment built up in the bottom of the gorge, and the river no longer washed down dead bodies. The mud and sand that had settled over the bones of the *Iguanodon* started to turn them to rock. Water trickling and seeping through the

ground filled empty spaces in the bones with minerals. These included silica and iron pyrite. (Silica is the main mineral of sand, and iron pyrite is a kind of iron ore.) This replacement of living matter with minerals is called fossilisation. It caused the shapes of the *Iguanodon* bones to be preserved for all time.

With other dinosaurs, their bones rotted away only after the sediment had turned to rock. They left holes in the rock called moulds. These filled up with minerals from rainwater and formed lumps in the shapes of the original bones. The lumps are known as casts. A few dinosaur fossils contained nothing of the original creatures – just their footprints where they had walked in mud.

▽ *Iguanodon* bodies washed down from the surrounding hills formed a dinosaur graveyard that was to remain hidden for millions of years.

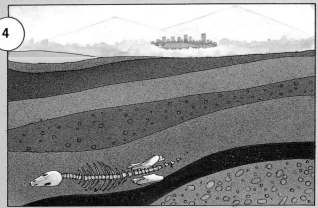

Turning dinosaurs into rocks

The body of a dead *Iguanodon* settles on the bottom of a river (1). It is buried by the mud and sand washed down, and its flesh rots away (2). Eventually other layers of sediment pile up above it. Forces and pressures within the crust, the skin of the Earth, turn these layers into beds of rock, and the bones are filled with minerals (3). Now the fossil skeleton lies hidden in the rocks below our feet (4). The whole process of fossilisation takes millions of years. Rock that is made up almost entirely of fossil bones is called a bone bed.

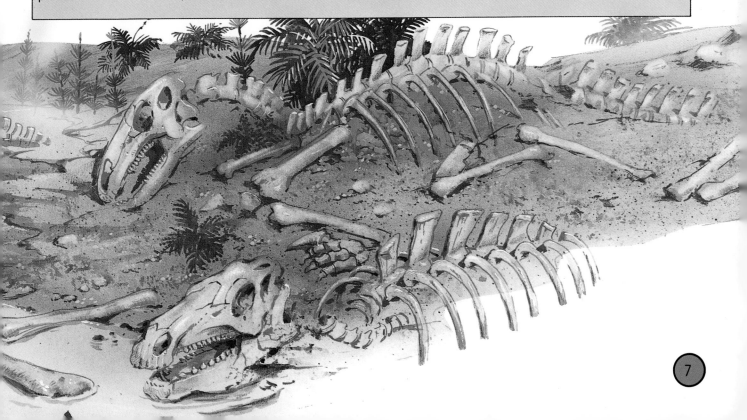

THE CHANGING LAND

It has been 140 million years since the *Iguanodon* bodies were deposited and buried. The ridge of rocks with the *Iguanodon* graveyard in the gorge was worn down by the weather, and a sea of warm water spread over the whole area for a while. The continents were continuing to move, and Africa began to push against Europe. In northern Europe this movement raised the land, and the shallow sea drained away. Forests grew everywhere, but as the climate gradually changed, these gave way to grasslands. By this time North America had broken away from Europe and the Atlantic Ocean had formed between them. Finally, in the last 2 million years or so, the landscape became as it is today.

While this had been happening, the animal life had changed. The dinosaurs had died out and the mammals had taken their place.

The first finds and early fossil hunters

This painting shows fossil hunters at a chalk pit in Cambridgeshire, eastern England, in 1822.
With the discovery of *Megalosaurus*, *Iguanodon* and fossils of other similar animals, scientists began to realise that a whole group of giant reptiles once walked the Earth. In 1842, British scientist Sir Richard Owen gave this group the name *Dinosauria*, meaning "terrible lizards".

About 250,000 years ago, one particular species of mammal, the first humans, moved into the area. As people began to explore their surroundings, they tried to make sense of the natural world. They developed ideas about how rocks were formed, and how the shells and bones of living things of the past were turned to stone and embedded in them.

The first recognisable dinosaur bones were discovered in eastern England early in the nineteenth century. The first dinosaur to be described and named was *Megalosaurus,* meaning great lizard. This was a big meat-eater. William Buckland, a scientist at Oxford University, did this work in 1824 based on a single fossil jawbone with teeth. The second dinosaur to be discovered was *Iguanodon* in 1825. But this, too, was in England, not in Belgium at the *Iguanodon* graveyard.

◁ The small town of Bernissart in south-west Belgium in the 1870s. This cut-away view of the coal mine below ground shows lift shafts and passages cut by miners through the layers of rock in order to reach and to dig out the coal. There are also objects buried in the rocks – the *Iguanodon* fossils or remains. Above ground are the mine buildings.

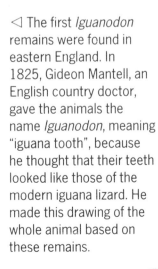

◁ The first *Iguanodon* remains were found in eastern England. In 1825, Gideon Mantell, an English country doctor, gave the animals the name *Iguanodon*, meaning "iguana tooth", because he thought that their teeth looked like those of the modern iguana lizard. He made this drawing of the whole animal based on these remains.

AWAITING DISCOVERY

The idea of dinosaurs became very popular in nineteenth-century Europe. The work of fossil hunters William Buckland on *Megalosaurus* and Gideon Mantell on *Iguanodon* caught the imagination of the public. In natural history books made at the time, illustrations of both these dinosaurs, shown as giant lizards, were often included. So, too, were illustrations of fossil sea reptiles, like the long-necked plesiosaurs and the fish-shaped ichthyosaurs. These extinct creatures had been known for a number of years.

In 1851 the Great Exhibition of the Works of Industry of All Nations was held in Hyde Park in London. The main exhibition hall was a huge structure of steel, glass and wood called the Crystal Palace. After the exhibition closed, the Crystal Palace was taken apart and put up again in a park in Sydenham, south London. The park was renamed Crystal Palace.

The first dinosaur theme park
In Crystal Palace Park in south London stand these concrete dinosaur statues. They were built in 1854 with instructions from English fossil hunter Sir Richard Owen. We now know that the animals did not look like this, but they were good models considering the little information on dinosaurs available at the time.

Miners discover strange shapes in the coal seam.

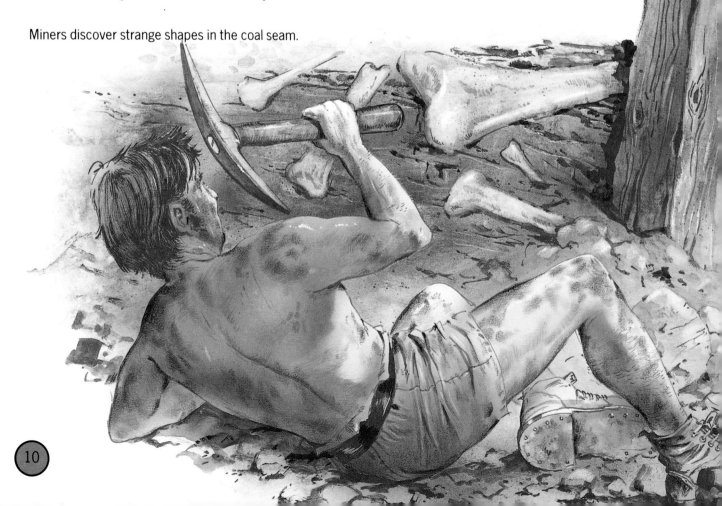

More evidence, new interpretations

In the grounds of Crystal Palace were placed full-sized statues of the dinosaurs and other fossil animals as they were known at the time. The Crystal Palace itself is long gone – destroyed in a fire in 1936 – but the beautiful dinosaur statues are still there.

The idea that dinosaurs were lizards built like elephants remained for some time. Then, in 1858, part of a dinosaur skeleton was found in New Jersey in the United States. It was studied by Joseph Leidy, professor of anatomy at the University of Pennsylvania, and he named it *Hadrosaurus,* meaning "thick lizard". It was similar to *Iguanodon,* but there was enough of the skeleton to show that in life it had not resembled an elephant-like lizard. Instead, it must have looked more like a kangaroo, standing on its long hind legs with its shorter front legs dangling before it.

In 1868, Benjamin Waterhouse Hawkins, the sculptor who had created the Crystal Palace statues, mounted the *Hadrosaurus* skeleton for Leidy at the Academy of Natural Sciences in Philadelphia, Pennsylvania – the first mounted dinosaur skeleton ever exhibited.

Shortly afterwards, in 1878, coal miners in Bernissart, Belgium, were tunnelling through a coal seam when the coal suddenly came to an end. Instead of coal they found clay filled with strange-looking lumps. The *Iguanodon* graveyard had been discovered.

△ A reconstruction of an *Iguanodon* found on the Isle of Wight, England, in 1917. It is one of the most complete dinosaur skeletons found in the British Isles.

FINISHING THE PUZZLE

The Belgian coal miner Jules Creteur, who found the oddly shaped lumps in the mine at Bernissart, brought them to the surface and examined them. He found that they were bits of fossilised bone. Creteur had been tunnelling through the rocks of the ancient ridge and had discovered the depression filled with Cretaceous sediments and the *Iguanodon* graveyard.

Mining work was stopped. A team from the Royal Museum of Natural History in Brussels was brought in, and experts began to dig out the skeletons. In three years, thirty-nine *Iguanodon* skeletons were brought up to the surface of the mine. These were mostly complete, unlike the earlier *Iguanodon* finds of Mantell and others in England.

The scientist best known for the dinosaur work done at Bernissart is Louis Dollo of the Royal Museum of Natural History, Brussels. In 1882 he began to study and reconstruct the skeletons. In Brussels, in a building that was once a chapel, he and his team mounted eleven of the most complete skeletons in life-like poses – a job that took 30 years. Dollo believed that *Iguanodon* probably moved about on its hind legs, unlike the modern iguana. The Belgian king of the time, Leopold II, visited the display and remarked

that the *Iguanodon* looked like giraffes, with their tall necks and small heads. In any case, the skeletons suggested an animal that was very different from the elephant-like lizards drawn by Mantell.

Dollo found that there were two different sizes of *Iguanodon*. He thought these may have represented two different species or types, or the males and females of just one species. We now believe that the first explanation was correct: there are several *Iguanodon* species.

▽ Once the skeletons were in Brussels, one of the researchers, G. Lavalette, made these drawings in the positions in which they were buried.

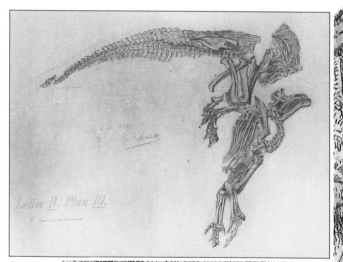

The fossil *Iguanodon* embedded in the rock.

▽ The complete *Iguanodon* skeletons were too large to be moved in single pieces. Mine workers and scientists sawed them up into blocks, then numbered the blocks, removed them from the ground and put them back together in order in the laboratory.

△ This painting, made from a photograph taken in 1889 by L. Becker, shows the first of the *Iguanodon* skeletons being put together in St. George's Chapel in Brussels. Even in its incomplete state, the animal's small head, massive tail and the shape of its limbs, were obvious.

DINOSAUR FEVER

While studies of *Iguanodon* were being carried out in Europe, the attention of many fossil hunters switched to North America, where many dinosaur finds were being made.

In 1877 a British fossil collector, Arthur Lakes, and a naval captain from Connecticut, H.C. Beckwith, found some big bones at the foot of the Rocky Mountains at Morrison, near Denver, Colorado. Lakes sent a message to Othniel Charles Marsh, professor of palaeontology at Yale University, asking for help. Marsh was slow to reply, so Lakes sent a similar message to the wealthy scientist and fossil collector Edward Drinker Cope in Philadelphia, Pennsylvania.

This sparked what were to become known as the Bone Wars. Cope and Marsh did not like one another. When Marsh realised that his rival and a team of palaeontologists were at Morrison, he sent out his own team to make new dinosaur discoveries. Both men realised that the site, which geologists call the Morrison Formation, was going to be rich in fossils. Both Cope and Marsh hired workers armed with guns and rifles, and each poached the other's men and their fossil finds. It is said that one team would take what they wanted from an area and smash up everything else so that the other team would not get it. Most of the fighting centred on a hill called Como Bluff in Wyoming. There, huge numbers of dinosaur fossils could be seen at the surface.

During the Bone Wars many dinosaur fossils may have been destroyed, but the wars did do some good. Both Cope and Marsh wanted to get their finds shown in museums as quickly as possible, so they developed a way of uncovering the bones without damaging them. They left each bone partly buried in the rock and covered it with plaster of Paris. Then they cut out a block of rock with the bone still in it. The bone was removed from the rock in a laboratory, where it was easier to work. This technique is still used today. By the late 1890s, many different dinosaurs had been discovered. Marsh had found, among others, *Stegosaurus* and *Allosaurus,* while Cope had found *Camarasaurus* and *Coelophysis.*

The dinosaur hunters
Edward Drinker Cope and Othniel Charles Marsh used their own money to pay for dinosaur expeditions. Later, rich businessmen, such as the Scottish-born American Andrew Carnegie, paid for the hunting, study and display in museums of dinosaur skeletons. Palaeontologists named *Diplodocus carnegii* after him and *Apatosaurus louisae* after his wife.

Edward Cope

Othniel Marsh

Andrew Carnegie

△ (Top) Dressed and armed for the dinosaur hunt, Marsh-centre of back row-and his men pose for the camera.

△ Arthur Lakes was not only a fossil hunter but also an artist. He painted this picture of Marsh's men at work at Como Bluff.

FINDING DINOSAURS

Exposed by science
Dinosaur skeletons are usually found by members of scientific expeditions who know in what types and ages of rocks to look for them.

Uncovered in deserts
The dry desert winds wear away the surface of rocks. The fossils of dinosaur footprints in the rocks are eventually exposed.

Washed out by rivers
A river wearing away a hillside will expose the different rock layers, or strata, of which the hill is made. Fossils in the strata will be uncovered.

Since the days of Cope and Marsh, the hunt for dinosaurs has spread to all the continents. In the early years of this century, many discoveries were made in Canada, particularly in Alberta. This work was pioneered by the American fossil hunter Barnum Brown and followed by C.H. Sternberg and his three sons. The skeletons they found filled museums in New York, Ottawa and Toronto.

Then Africa became the centre for dinosaur discoveries. Between 1909 and 1929, in what is now Tanzania, German and British expeditions found dinosaurs like those of the Morrison Formation. In the 1920s, American expeditions to Mongolia found several fossil dinosaurs, including the first dinosaur eggs. In the 1970s and 1980s, spectacular dinosaur discoveries came from Mongolia, China and South America. Recent finds have been in the United States, Canada, England, Greenland, Australia and Antarctica.

DINOSAURS ALL AROUND THE WORLD
Dinosaur remains have been found on all continents.

- Triassic fossils
- Early and Middle Jurassic fossils
- Late Jurassic fossils
- Early Cretaceous fossils
- Late Cretaceous fossils

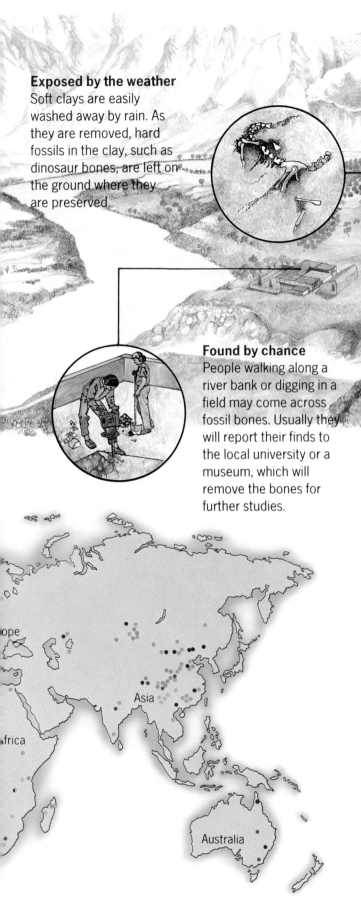

Exposed by the weather
Soft clays are easily washed away by rain. As they are removed, hard fossils in the clay, such as dinosaur bones, are left on the ground where they are preserved.

Found by chance
People walking along a river bank or digging in a field may come across fossil bones. Usually they will report their finds to the local university or a museum, which will remove the bones for further studies.

ope

Asia

frica

Australia

ntarctica

Today, palaeontologists may set out to explore remote places where dinosaur bones are known to be common. These fossil hunts can be as dramatic as those in the days of Cope and Marsh. The most important part of such a trip is the preparation. A dinosaur-hunting expedition can cost tens of thousands of pounds. It may take many years to persuade governments and universities that it is money well spent and that they should pay for the trip. Politics may be a problem, too. Often the new dinosaur sites are situated in developing countries where there are civil wars or conflicts between neighbouring peoples. These peoples are likely to be suspicious of foreigners digging around in their lands. In 1977, for instance, scientists on the International Palaeontological Expedition to Nigeria spent Christmas in a Nigerian prison because the local people did not believe they were simply fossil hunting.

DIGGING UP THE PAST

Once a dinosaur skeleton has been found, a team of expert fossil hunters moves in. The team tries to find out the type of dinosaur the skeleton came from and how best to remove the bones from the ground.

At first, usually only part of the skeleton is seen. Perhaps someone finds a piece of bone at the foot of a slope and reports this discovery to a museum, which immediately sends a palaeontologist to investigate. The palaeontologist searches the cliffs above the slope to see from where the bone fragment fell. He or she finds more bones in a bed of rock exposed on the cliff-face. He concludes that the rest of the skeleton must lie deep within the rocks of the cliff.

Unearthing the skeleton

The fossil hunters use small bulldozers and excavators to clear away the rocks above the bed containing the skeleton. When they have dug down close to the skeleton, the earth-moving machines are taken away and the rest of the rock material above the fossils is carefully cleared by hand. As each part of the skeleton is uncovered, it is measured, drawn and photographed.

If the skeleton is buried in solid rock, the whole rock bed is cut up into large blocks, which are carried by truck to the museum. If the skeleton lies in soft material like clay, however, the team clears away the clay above the bones by hand. The exposed bones are

▽ Although fossil bones are made of mineral and have existed for hundreds of millions of years, they are very fragile. They must be protected by being filled with resin or coated with plaster of Paris or fibreglass, as here, before being transported to the museum.

◁ Once a fossil skeleton has been exposed, the first job is to get it under cover. It needs to be protected from the weather, which can break down some of the minerals in the fossils.

coated with wet paper and then with bandages or cloth soaked in plaster of Paris. When the top surface of each bone is completely coated and protected, the clay underneath is scraped away. The bone is then turned over and the newly exposed side treated in the same way. The bone packages can then be carried off safely to the museum for the detailed work on the fossils.

Uncovering the bones

The palaeontologists examine tiny fossils and structures in the rock itself as well as the bones, in order to build up a picture of the landscape in which the dinosaur lived.

Back at the museum, technicians known as preparators carefully remove the protective plaster cases or the rock containing the bones. They use power tools like dentist's drills for grinding or cutting away the rock. For delicate work, they use fine dental probes and even pins and sewing needles. Sometimes the preparators use chemicals to dissolve away the rock, or sound waves to shake the bones free. When their work is complete the bones are ready for the palaeontologists to study.

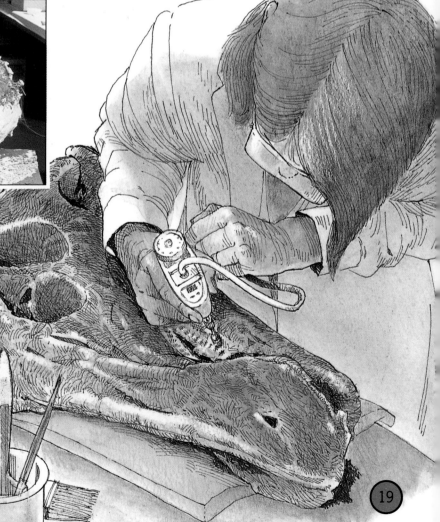

△▷ At the museum or laboratory, the protective casing is removed, as is any rock around the fossils. This process may take years, especially if acid has to be used to eat away the rock from around the bones. The acid is applied by brush or medicine dropper. Fossil preparation is very skilled, slow work.

THE BONES OF A DINOSAUR

If a dinosaur skeleton removed from rocks or the ground is almost complete, then the museum may decide to put it on display instead of keeping it in the laboratory for detailed study. (Only rarely are complete dinosaur skeletons found.)

Before any of this is done, however, the scientists must know the structure of the animal when it was alive – how its bones were joined together, how the joints moved and whether it stood on two or four legs.

Making a dinosaur display is like building a skyscraper. A steel framework is built to support the skeleton. If the bones are too delicate to handle, a copy of the skeleton is made and this is displayed instead. First, a mould and cast are made of each bone. Then the casts are mounted, and arranged as a skeleton on the framework in a lifelike pose.

△ Sometimes, fossil dinosaur bones are so jumbled, like these of an *Iguanodon*, that they must be fitted together like a jigsaw puzzle to make a reconstruction.

The casts can be made with plaster, as in Andrew Carnegie's *Diplodocus* skeleton. He had ten copies made of all 300 bones and gave the skeletons as gifts to museums around the world. Nowadays, though, more lightweight materials are used, such as hollow fibreglass. The Museum of Natural History in Denver, Colorado, has a 12-metre-long *Tyrannosaurus* skeleton that is so light it stands on one leg.

If a display dinosaur has any bones missing, casts of these are made from the bones of other skeletons of the same species. Or a palaeontologist makes casts based on what he or she thinks they may have looked like.

Tail of Deinonychus with interlocking bony bars

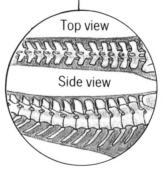

Top view

Side view

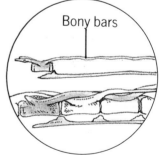

Bony bars

Side to side, or up and down? The tail of *Allosaurus* was tall and narrow. This suggests that it could move its tail from side to side more easily than it could move it up and down.

Flexible or stiff? The tail bones of some dinosaurs were surrounded by very long bony bars, making the tail rigid. This is not the case in *Allosaurus*.

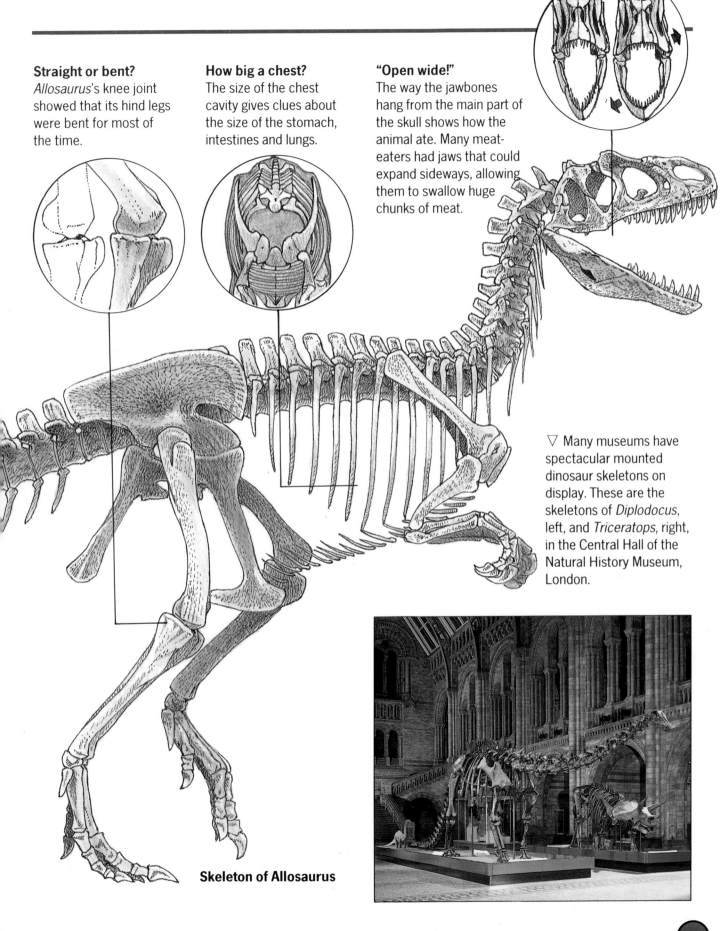

Straight or bent?
Allosaurus's knee joint showed that its hind legs were bent for most of the time.

How big a chest?
The size of the chest cavity gives clues about the size of the stomach, intestines and lungs.

"Open wide!"
The way the jawbones hang from the main part of the skull shows how the animal ate. Many meat-eaters had jaws that could expand sideways, allowing them to swallow huge chunks of meat.

▽ Many museums have spectacular mounted dinosaur skeletons on display. These are the skeletons of *Diplodocus*, left, and *Triceratops*, right, in the Central Hall of the Natural History Museum, London.

Skeleton of Allosaurus

FLESH ON THE BONES

The skeleton is only the starting-point for restoring or making a copy of an extinct animal such as a dinosaur. It is just the supporting structure on which the living animal was built. The rest of the body, being made of soft tissues, never fossilised. The task of the scientist is to rebuild the complete animal from whatever clues and evidence he or she can find.

The first step is to put muscles on the bare bones. Here the bones themselves can provide some clues. In life the muscles were attached to the bones by tendons, and these sometimes left marks where they were connected to the

bones. Next, a knowledge of engineering and construction is used. The scientist needs to understand what forces the dinosaur would have needed to move the various parts of its body. He or she needs to know how the bones could work as levers and pivots. From this the scientist can work out how the muscles would have been arranged to produce those forces.

With muscles over the bones, it is possible to get a good idea of the overall shape and size of the dinosaur. However, for a complete restoration, the scientist has to work out how parts of the body deep beneath the skin were organised. This requires an understanding of

▷ Building up a complete picture of a dinosaur requires not only the making of a model or a mounted skeleton but also an understanding of the shape and structure of the dinosaur's body, how the animal lived and how it behaved.

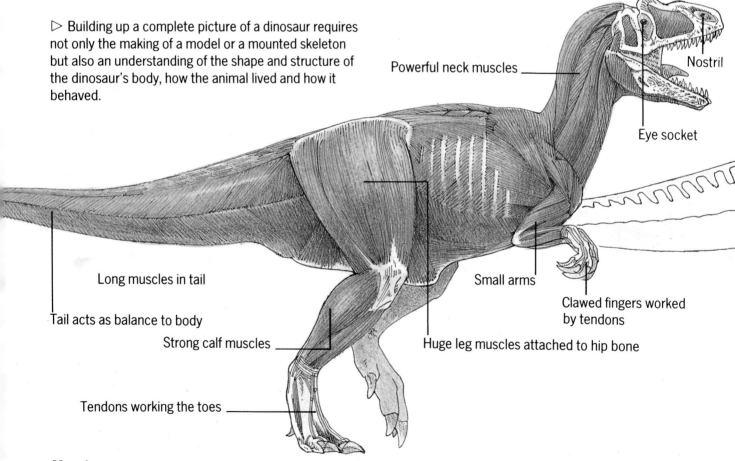

Powerful neck muscles

Nostril

Eye socket

Long muscles in tail

Tail acts as balance to body

Strong calf muscles

Tendons working the toes

Small arms

Clawed fingers worked by tendons

Huge leg muscles attached to hip bone

Muscles
Leg muscles in an enormous two-footed animal like this dinosaur must have been very large. Those needed to move its small forelimbs would have been less powerful. The muscles attached to each bone of its tail would have

been quite small. There are no fossils of dinosaur muscles but the palaeontologist can estimate the size of muscle needed for each action or movement and build up the restoration from this information.

the habits and behaviour of the dinosaur – its lifestyle. For this, a mixture of guesswork and experience is used. Some scientists will think that the animal was warm-blooded, others that it was cold-blooded. If it had been warm-blooded, it would have needed a great deal of energy. The heart and the lungs would have had to be very large, like those of an elephant. The lungs may have been small but efficient, with extra air sacs to take as much oxygen as possible from each breath, as do the lungs of modern birds. As a cold-blooded animal, it would have needed only small lungs, more like those of a crocodile.

▷ (Photo above right) Fossil vertebrae (backbones) and strap-like tendons of a *Tyrannosaurus*.

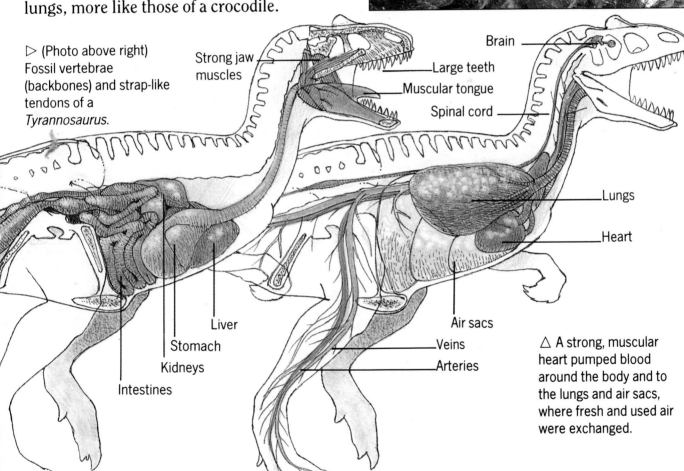

Brain

Large teeth

Strong jaw muscles

Muscular tongue

Spinal cord

Lungs

Heart

Liver

Stomach

Air sacs

Kidneys

Veins

Arteries

Intestines

△ A strong, muscular heart pumped blood around the body and to the lungs and air sacs, where fresh and used air were exchanged.

The digestive organs

The guts – the stomach and intestines – of a meat-eating dinosaur would have been much smaller than the large complex guts needed to break down and get nutrients from plant food. We know this from looking at present-day meat-eating animals, such as cats and dogs, and plant-eating animals, such as cows and rabbits. Comparison with modern animals is a very important part of restoring and reconstructing a dinosaur's body.

THE COMPLETE DINOSAUR

The final stage in dinosaur restoration probably requires the most imagination – putting the skin on the animal and giving this a colour scheme.

For most dinosaurs we have no idea what their skins were like. For a few, we do have skin impressions, which are marks made as skin is pressed into soft ground. The impressions may have been formed as the animal was buried quickly under mud or clay and the sediments picked up the texture of the skin before it rotted away. Over millions of years, these marks were turned to rock.

Deciding on the skin colour is more difficult. There is no evidence available. We believe that dinosaurs had good eyesight and could see colours, so we can be fairly sure that skin colour played a part in their lives. Big showy bumps on the head, called crests, as well

Skin colour and camouflage
The stripes on this *Allosaurus* restoration are based on those of the tiger. An animal with the same lifestyle may have had a similar colour scheme.

as sail-like structures on the back, were all probably very colourful. The dinosaurs would have used these as signals. Hunting dinosaurs may have had striped or spotted skins so that they could creep up on their prey unnoticed. Plant-eating animals may well have been camouflaged, with dark colours above and light colours below. Their young may have been striped or dappled so that their colours blended in with sunlit areas and shadows of their nests in the undergrowth. We can only make comparisons with the colour schemes of modern animals. What helps today's creatures survive may also have worked for dinosaurs.

Skin texture
The only meat-eating dinosaur for which we have a sample of skin texture is the South American *Carnotaurus*. Most of the skin had a fine scaly texture like a lizard's or snake's, but it also had rows of big scales, like low cones, running the length of the body. *Allosaurus* may have had skin with a similar texture. It is even possible that the smaller meat-eaters were covered with feathers.

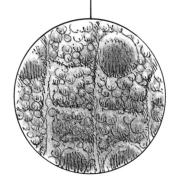

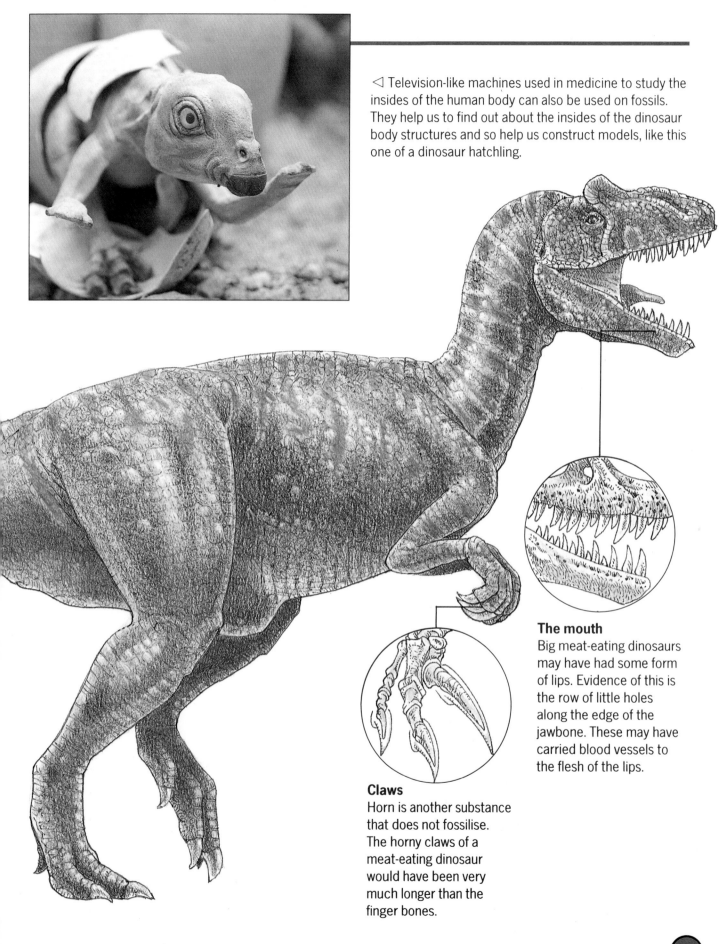

◁ Television-like machines used in medicine to study the insides of the human body can also be used on fossils. They help us to find out about the insides of the dinosaur body structures and so help us construct models, like this one of a dinosaur hatchling.

The mouth
Big meat-eating dinosaurs may have had some form of lips. Evidence of this is the row of little holes along the edge of the jawbone. These may have carried blood vessels to the flesh of the lips.

Claws
Horn is another substance that does not fossilise. The horny claws of a meat-eating dinosaur would have been very much longer than the finger bones.

CONSTRUCTING A LIFE

Even after the body of the dinosaur has been restored, the job of the fossil hunter is only half done. The animal's lifestyle, its fellow creatures and its surroundings must also be reconstructed in order to create a complete picture of the living animal. Detective work is used to finish this puzzle.

A famous example of a dinosaur puzzle rests in Wyoming. The fossil of a broken *Camarasaurus* skeleton lies exposed on a shelf of sandstone and limestone rock. The softer rock, siltstone, that once covered the dinosaur has been worn away. *Camarasaurus* was a long-necked plant-eater and was common in the area in Late Jurassic times. Among the scattered bones are the broken teeth of the big meat-eating dinosaur *Ceratosaurus* and the small meat-eater *Ornitholestes*. The *Camarasaurus* bones are scored with deep toothmarks, mostly the size of the teeth of *Allosaurus,* another meat-eater.

From these details the palaeontologists have worked out a possible story: The *Camarasaurus* lived on a dry plain, since the special mix of limestone and sandstone in the shelf is found only in this type of landscape. One *Camarasaurus* moved away from the main herd and was attacked and killed by an *Allosaurus*. Once the *Allosaurus* had eaten its meal, it moved off. The remains of the *Camarasaurus* were set upon by a group of scavenging *Ceratosaurus*. What was left was finished off by the packs of *Ornitholestes* that had been waiting around like jackals while the bigger animals took the tastiest pieces. Not long afterwards a nearby river flooded, covering the plain and the skeleton with silt. This gradually became the siltstone that lay on top of the fossils.

There are other explanations, but the fossil site does show the interaction between the dinosaurs that lived there long ago.

▽ An *Allosaurus* feasts on a young *Camarasaurus*. The clues to this ancient murder lie scattered through the rocks in which the victim is fossilised.

The bones can tell us what kind of animal was killed, and marks on them can reveal what killed it and how.

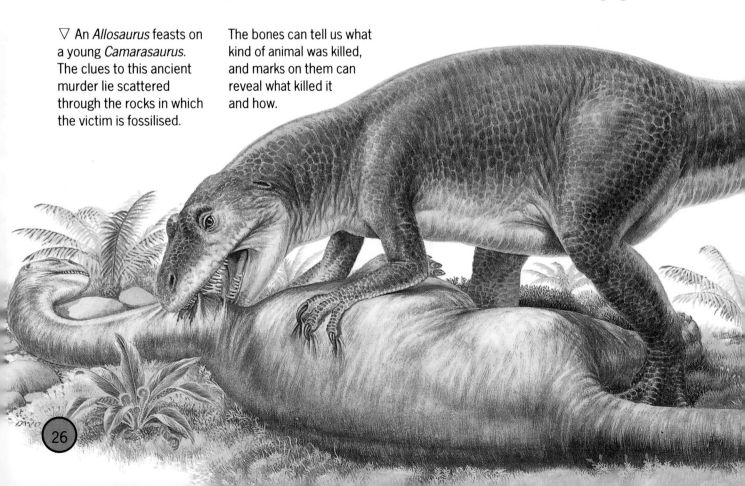

△ Modern museum reconstructions and restorations, like this one at Dallas (Texas) Science Museum, try to show not only the animal but also its surroundings and its lifestyle. They try to present the known facts as a completed jigsaw-puzzle picture.

▷ Technicians producing robotic dinosaurs for display in museums. When we look at reconstructions like these, we can create in our own minds pictures of ancient landscapes and living creatures.

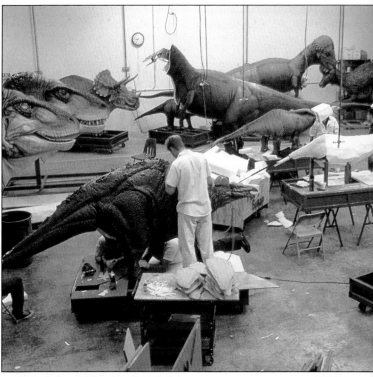

A FASCINATION WITH DINOSAURS

Why do we find dinosaurs so fascinating and such fun? It is probably for the same reasons that we like stories of monsters and dragons. We are interested in things that are strange and frightening. We enjoy imagining what they were or could be like.

Ever since the fossilised bones were recognised for what they were, and the name *dinosaur* was created, almost 150 years ago, the idea of extinct monsters has gripped people's imaginations and interest. Younger children can pronounce the creatures' names before they can read and write. Dinosaur displays are among the most popular parts of museums. Dinosaurs appear in comic strips, as toys, as badges, as advertising logos, in the form of biscuits and on postage stamps.

Ever since the Crystal Palace sculptures were built in 1854 there have been dinosaur theme parks. In 1907, concrete dinosaurs were built for Hagenbeck's Zoo in Hamburg, Germany. The most recent development has been the building of full-sized dinosaur models that move.

Dinosaurs have always been popular in the works of literature, from Jules Verne's *Journey to the Centre of the Earth* to the most modern science-fiction novels like Michael Crichton's *Jurassic Park*. They have also appeared in films. The spectacular images produced on cinema screens lend themselves well to visions of fantastic creatures. *King Kong,* made in 1933, was the dinosaur classic of the first talking motion pictures. Later dinosaur successes included *One Million Years B.C.* and *The Land That Time Forgot.* The film makers used models, costumed actors and lizards fitted with horns and sails as animated dinosaurs to give us a glimpse of a world that has long gone.

△ The latest in dinosaur technology – a robotic *Triceratops* that can move its head and make sounds. Exhibits like this help us imagine the world of dinosaurs.

◁ The fossil skeleton of a dinosaur lies buried in the ground. It is evidence of a creature that lived more than 140 million years ago when the world was a very different place from how it is today.

DO YOU KNOW?

What is the biggest mounted dinosaur skeleton?

The mounted skeleton of *Brachiosaurus* in the Humboldt Museum in Berlin is 22 metres long. It stands 6 metres high at the shoulders, and the head is carried 12 metres above the ground.

What is the tallest mounted dinosaur skeleton?

A skeleton of *Barosaurus,* a long-necked plant-eater like *Diplodocus,* stands in the American Museum of Natural History in New York City. Rearing up on its hind legs, its head is 17 metres above the floor of the museum.

What is the longest set of fossil footprints?

In Late Jurassic rocks of Colorado there is a run of *Apatosaurus* footprints that goes continuously for a distance of 215 metres.

What country has yielded the most types of dinosaurs?

More genera of dinosaurs have been found in the United States than in any other country – 64 at the last count. This is followed closely by Mongolia, with 40, China with 36, Canada with 31, and the United Kingdom with 26.

What is the biggest dinosaur bone discovered so far?

The biggest bone is the solid hip structure of a long-necked plant-eater found in Colorado in 1988, close to where the remains of *Supersaurus* and *Ultrasaurus* were discovered in the late 1970s. This structure, consisting of the hip bones and the vertebrae (back bones) attached to it, measures 1.8 metres high and 1.35 metres long, and weighs 675 kilograms.

Did any dinosaurs survive beyond the Cretaceous Period?

Now and again fossil dinosaur-like teeth are found in rocks that date from after the end of the Cretaceous Period 65 million years ago. Some of the teeth belonged to a kind of land-living crocodile and not to a dinosaur at all. Others are yet to be identified. A number of scientists say that birds evolved from dinosaurs, so although dinosaurs are extinct, their descendants are all around us today.

What is the smallest dinosaur footprint found?

A three-toed footprint less than 2.5 centimetres long, probably from a meat-eater, was found by an amateur collector in the Early Jurassic rocks of Nova Scotia in Canada. The animal that made it must have been about the size of a sparrow.

What was the first mounted dinosaur skeleton?

The plaster cast of the *Hadrosaurus* skeleton mounted by Waterhouse Hawkins under Joseph Leidy's direction in the Academy of Natural Sciences in Philadelphia in 1868 was the first ever on display.

What was the first dinosaur film?

The first dinosaur film was a silent cartoon film called *Gertie the Dinosaur,* made by Windsor McCay in 1912. Gertie was, in fact, the first character ever to be designed for a cartoon. The first animated model dinosaur was an *Apatosaurus* filmed in 1914 by Willis O'Brien, who later animated the dinosaurs for *The Lost World* made in (1925) and *King Kong* (1933).

GLOSSARY

anatomy The study of the structure of living things – for example, how a dinosaur's bones fitted together, and the size and shape of the various parts of its body.

camouflaged Coloured in such a way that the animal blends in, or merges, with its background so that it will not be noticed.

coal A rock made from the remains of ancient plants that were buried and squashed by mud, silt and sand being laid on top of them.

cold-blooded The term used to describe an animal that cannot control the temperature of its body – for example, a fish.

conifer A tree such as a pine or a redwood that has seeds in cones and needle-like leaves.

cycads Plants like palm trees that bear clusters of leaves at the top that resemble the fronds of ferns.

fibreglass Glass in the form of very fine strands. When mixed with glue-like materials, it forms a very tough and lightweight substance.

fossilisation The process of the remains of living things being turned into rock, forming fossils.

fossils Any parts or traces of living things of long ago that are preserved in the rocks.

horn A tough, shiny substance made of the same chemical material as finger nails and hair, and often formed as a protective covering on some part of an animal. The name is also used for a structure covered with horn, like that of a cow.

horsetails Non-flowering plants related to the ferns that have a straight stem with clusters of narrow leaves. They were abundant when dinosaurs first evolved, as were ferns.

ichthyosaurs Swimming reptiles of Triassic, Jurassic and Cretaceous times that were so adapted to life in the water that they looked like modern dolphins.

limestone A rock made up mainly of the mineral calcite. Some limestones are formed from the calcite of shells of sea animals that died long ago and were buried on the sea bed.

minerals Substances formed naturally in the ground of which all rocks are made. They include mixtures of elements such as iron, aluminium, potassium, carbon, silicon, oxygen and hydrogen.

moulds Hollow containers, each having the shape of a particular object into which a liquid is poured. When the liquid hardens, it takes the object's shape. The copy of the object is known as a cast.

palaeontologists Scientists that study palaeontology, the science of fossils and living things of the past.

plaster of Paris A mixture of fine powder and water that sets hard. It is used to make casts in pottery and also to protect a person's broken bones until they have healed.

plesiosaurs Swimming reptiles from the Age of Dinosaurs that had squat bodies, paddles as limbs and either long necks and small heads or short necks and big heads.

prey An animal that is hunted and eaten by a meat-eater, a predator.

pterosaurs Flying reptiles related to the dinosaurs. They flew using a wing of skin. They lived during the Triassic, Jurassic and Cretaceous periods.

reconstruction The skeleton of an animal rebuilt from its bones or casts of the bones.

restoration A picture or a model of an animal as it appeared in life. This may include showing the surroundings of the animal.

sandstone A rock formed from sand particles cemented together.

scavenger A meat-eating animal that does not make its own kills but eats the bodies of other animals already dead.

sediment Tiny pieces of soil, earth or rock – for example, grains of sand or specks of mud that are deposited at the bottom of the sea or on a river bed.

silt A sediment that is finer than sand but coarser or rougher than mud.

siltstone Rock formed from silt particles cemented together by pressure from layers of more sediment from above.

tendon A strap or sheet of fibrous tissue that connects a muscle to a bone.

warm-blooded Term used to describe an animal that can regulate its own body temperature – for example, a mammal or a bird.

INDEX

ACKNOWLEDGEMENTS

Picture credits
Page 8 Ann Ronan Picture Library. Page 9 The Natural History Museum,
London. Page 10 Dr. Pat Morris. Page 11 The Natural History Museum,
London. Pages 12, 13 Department of Paleontology, Royal Belgian Institute
of Natural Sciences, Brussels. Page 15 (top and right) Yale Peabody
Museum of Natural History. Page 15 (bottom left) Mary Evans Picture
Library. Pages 18, 19 The Natural History Museum, London. Pages 20, 21
The Natural History Museum, London. Page 23 Dr. Pat Morris. Page 25
John Cancalosi/Bruce Coleman Limited Page 27 (both) Peter

Menzel/Science Photo Library. Page 28/29 The Natural History Museum,
London. Page 29 The Natural History Museum, London.

Artwork credits
Chris Forsey: pages 1, 2-3, 4-5, 6-7, 8-9, 10-11. James G. Robins: pages
12-13, 14, 18, 19, 20-21, 22-23, 24-25. Denys Ovenden: pages 26-27.
Hayward Art Group: pages 16-17 and diagrams on pages 4, 7. Steve Kirk:
cover illustration.